Handbook for Multi-Nee
Volume One
by Linda Williams

Contents

A Word From The Author

Hi there,

I have always had a love of crafts, but this wonderful hobby that we share quickly became a long-lasting passion. Parchment crafters seem to have a special affinity which crosses many language barriers, and through learning and progressing with the craft, I have made many special friends. If you are reading this book then you are either an avid parchment craft enthusiast like me, a complete beginner, or a totally hooked Groovi addict! I must admit, part of me is the latter too! Whichever it is, we all have one thing in common: the desire to craft and produce beautiful parchment creations. Which path you take to achieve this does not

matter in the slightest. What does matter is that it gives you, as a crafter, the greatest of pleasure. Whatever category you fit, this book is for you. There is something for everyone.

So it is with the greatest pleasure that I present to you the Pergamano Handbook for Multi-Needle Tools. It has been some time in the making, as we at Clarity/Pergamano wanted this book to be something special: a combination of both the traditional and new.

My greatest pleasure is using multi-needle tools to create the delicate lacework that is often seen in parchment craft, and I want to share with you everything I know about this. These techniques are easy and within reach of a beginner, but are also suitable for all levels of ability. The borders and lacework are straightforward, and range from simple to the more advanced.

If you are a complete beginner, then the comprehensive instructions on how to use multi-needle tools will be invaluable. There is also a detailed section on cutting. For the traditional enthusiast, there is a library of needle tool patterns for you to play with and use with your parchment creations. For the Groovi lovers, the projects included at the back of the book will interest you. Maybe you are a Groovi enthusiast who wants to expand your parchment knowledge and learn the more traditional techniques? Whatever drives you,

I am hopeful that each and every section will spark your enthusiasm.

I would like to thank my dear friend Barbara Gray and all the team at Clarity, firstly for the opportunity to make this book, and also for all the help in its production. A special mention must go to Jim Molloy, who is Chief Designer at Clarity headquarters. Jim was responsible for the photography and the layout of the book; we have spent days together getting it right. So thank you Jim for your incredible patience, creativity and expert knowledge. What a talent!

I hope this book inspires you to make your own beautiful parchment creations, and encourages you to experiment. Go for it and enjoy!

Linda Williams

xx

5

The Art of Parchment Craft

Parchment craft is a beautiful art form which consists of many various and interesting techniques.

Perforating is an integral part of this lovely craft, and this forms the basis of the traditional lacework that is found in parchment craft. Perforating, incorporated with good embossing and cutting, makes it possible to create all sorts of wonderful and intricate designs on parchment paper. The possibilities are endless.

There are a few simple guidelines to follow, to ensure you master the art of producing the realistic lacework that is synonymous with the craft.

The Art of Parchment Craft
Lacework

There are many ways to achieve good lacework. Gridwork is one such technique. This is where you have a grid with a uniform number of holes, either in a straight or diagonal configuration. You can then perforate through these holes, following a counting pattern, and then emboss freehand.

Another option is to do it freehand with the use of the multi-needle tools. This is my favourite way of producing lacework. Pergamano have produced many multi-needle tools, ranging from one needle up to twelve needles, all in different configurations. They can be used alone in a project, or combined with each other to produce the most stunning and varied patterns.

Alternatively, you can emboss dots using the grid, or a combination of both. This produces a very uniform looking piece of lacework.

The Art of Parchment Craft
Lacework

The perforating technique is usually done prior to embossing, (unless you are only using a 2-needle tool to make a picot edge along an embossed line) and always before the cutting out. The more accurately you perforate, the prettier and better your cutting will look. You can perforate by eye, within or around your design, or alternatively you can use one of the widely available patterns. There are a few basic rules to follow...

Firstly, you should rub your tumble dryer sheet over the back of your parchment before you start, as once the parchment has been perforated, the surface on the back of the parchment becomes rough.

Place your work onto the thin Groovi perforating mat, right side uppermost, as you will need to shallow perforate to start. The reason for this is that you will probably want to emboss some dots or shapes between your perforations, as this is a characteristic of good lacework.

If the holes are too big at this stage, the paper will be weakened and it may tear. Also, the embossing may flatten the holes slightly, but this is not a problem as you will re-perforate later.

Always ensure you perforate with your needle tool in an upright position at 90 degrees to the parchment paper. Using a Groovi Guard, as shown in the photograph, keeps the parchment flat and protects your work.

Using Multi-Needle Tools
A General Introduction

Perforating with a multi-needle tool to form a lace edge or lace insert

This can be done by eye, or you can follow a pattern. When you are creating multi-needle tool lace on your project, there are a few things to remember.

Using a paper pattern

If you are following a pattern, you should first photocopy it, so that your original will remain in pristine condition. Attach your parchment to your pattern copy using Groovi tabs. Place onto a thin perforating mat. With the multi-needle tool of your choice, begin perforating around the outer border, or the desired area within your project, perforating through both the parchment and the pattern at the same time. This will ensure accuracy, as the needle tool pattern will already be mapped out for you on the pattern.

All the patterns in this book are actual size and ergonomically placed for easy photocopying.

Perforating freehand, without the use of a pattern

This can be a little more challenging, and is best used for perforating along a straight line, around the border of a project or randomly to fill a space within a design. You can either use the repeat insertion technique, i.e. once you have done your first set of perforations with the multi-needle tool, the next perforation should be done by inserting the first needle of the tool into the last hole of the previous perforations.

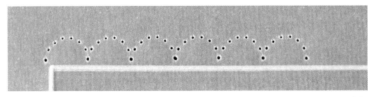

Alternatively, you can leave a small gap (about the width of a 2-needle tool) between each perforated group. You can either use a 2-needle tool for this, or do it by eye. When your work is cut out you will not notice this. Continue in this way until you have completed your perforations.

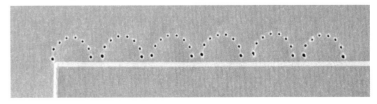

Using Multi-Needle Tools
A General Introduction

How to make a needle tool border fit

I quite often get asked this question. A needle tool is a certain length and a border might be a certain length, so how do you get them to fit exactly without leaving a noticeable gap?

This is the way I do it:

Perforate about three quarters of the way along your line, using the repeat insertion or by leaving a slight gap - it's up to you. Then you need to stop and calculate if it's all going to fit nicely. Usually it doesn't! Now do a trial run, carrying on along your line with the needle tool, but don't perforate, just mark the paper ever so slightly with the first and last needles if you can. If you press very gently (don't perforate) you will get a tiny white dot. When you get to the end, you will have a good idea as to how much you fall short or have overshot your line.

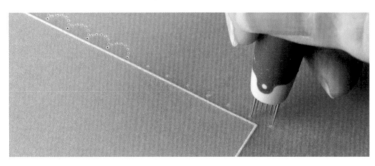

Now you need to adjust your perforations, by adding small gaps between the needle tool perforations in order to make it all fit perfectly.

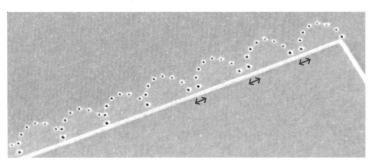

Once you have embossed, re-perforated and cut out your lacework, these gaps will not be noticeable.

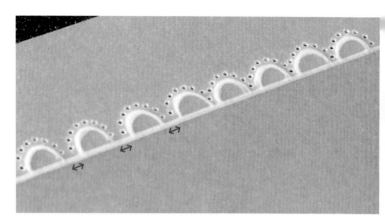

It's trial and error, but the more you do this, the better you will become at it!

As you can see here, once finished, the gaps are hardly noticeable.

Using Multi-Needle Tools
A General Introduction

Embossing within lacework

Now emboss on your embossing mat. You can trace your shapes in first, using a white pencil, which you can rub out after the first emboss. Alternatively, you can do them freehand, which is easy enough if you are just doing dots and ovals or simple shapes.

 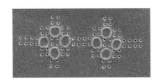

Usually you will need one of the smaller tools for this: I find the 3mm or the 1.5mm is a good choice. See which suits you best, then choose the largest appropriate embossing tool that will fit in the area to start off your embossing. Embossing rules still apply here, even though you are only embossing relatively small areas. The embossing, which is generally done on the back of the project, raises the paper, creating an impression of relief.

As the paper is gradually stretched, it changes into a soft white colour, and the more it is embossed the whiter it becomes. This must be done in stages, letting the paper rest in between. Where possible, leave the paper to rest overnight. When you are embossing dots or shapes within needle tool perforations, they should always fill the space nicely, and be equal in size. Good lacework has lots of nice bright white embossing within and there is usually very little visual evidence of the grey parchment...

Embossing a Dot

Select the correct ball tool for the size of dot that you want to create. The 3mm ball tool makes a nice sized dot. For a nice round shape, work gently from side to side, then up and down (when you feel the paper beginning to give), then go round and round. This avoids a black dot in the middle.

When embossing a dot within the perforations of a 4-needle tool, you will need to use the 1.0mm ball tool, but very carefully.

Once you have the combination of desired white dots or shapes, it's time to re-perforate.

Re-perforating

This is done to open up the holes so that the tips of your scissors or snips can be inserted without ripping the parchment paper. It re-opens any holes that have been flattened by your embossing and gives your embossing and crosses a neat, even appearance.

Place your work on the thicker perforating pad, with the right side uppermost. Perforate deeply this time, inserting the needles further into the parchment paper. Take care, as misalignment will create multiple holes which will reduce the quality of the finished piece. If you cannot reinsert the tool in exactly the same place, then perforate deeply using a 1-needle tool. This can be more time consuming, but will be more accurate, thus resulting in much neater work. If you need to have bigger holes, you can use the 1-needle bold.

You can now cut out as required. If you have a paper pattern, the correct cutting will be indicated by a red V shape situated between two black dots, which will indicate the space between two perforations.

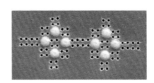 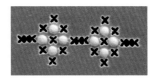

Fancy!

This intricate lacework is made using only the 4-Needle tool and Semi-Circle Tool.

Using Multi-Needle Tools

The possibilities are infinite and please don't limit yourself to just my choice. By taking one small design, adding your own embossing in chosen places and cutting out the parts that you want, you can design a piece of lace that will look totally different to mine.

I could give one corner to ten different people and you would not believe that the work that they produced had originated from the same pattern!

Go on... experiment! What have you got to lose? At best you will have designed something yourself, at worst a piece of paper will end up in the bin! A top tip though: always try out on a scrap first. Don't go trying on your best piece of work.

The merits of the 1-needle bold

The 1-needle bold is a useful tool and has specific uses. As the name suggests, it makes a bigger, more pronounced hole than the standard 1-needle tool.

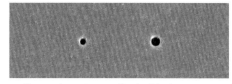

1-needle tool vs 1-needle bold size comparison.

The 1-needle bold is good for using with the bold grids, the standard 1-needle is ideal for fine grids. It also fills the space well within the star embossing tool, to make a nice decorative feature, and is great for stippling.

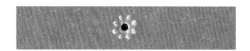

Numerous patterns from just one tool

On the pattern sheets that follow, you will find a sheet representing each Pergmano needle tool. The sheet will include multiple combinations that you can photocopy and use as borders and patterns within your projects. Also, there will be a picture of the work that I have done using the patterns.

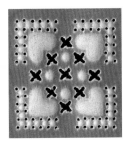
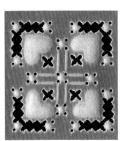
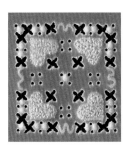

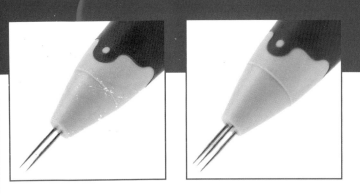

2-Needle Tool PER-TO-70037-XX (10261)

3-Needle Tool PER-TO-70038-XX (10281)

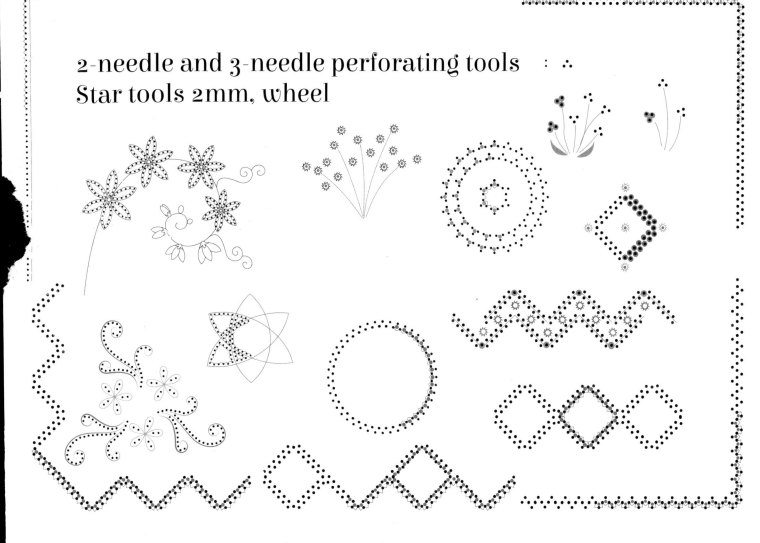

2-needle and 3-needle perforating tools
Star tools 2mm, wheel

● Perforate   ● Emboss   ⌄ Cut

2-Needle & 3-Needle Tools

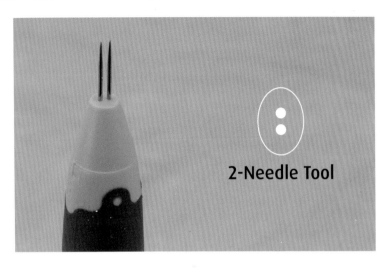

2-Needle Tool

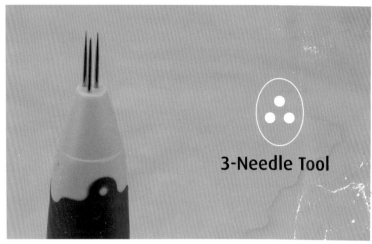

3-Needle Tool

Perforating with a 2 Needle tool to form a picot edge

To create a neatly cut picot edge, use a 2-needle perforating tool along a line that is already embossed (you can perforate deeply in this case). This is because you have no further embossing to do in and around the perforations, and as your line is already embossed, there is no need to perforate shallow. This forms relatively large holes that make it easier to insert the points of your scissors.

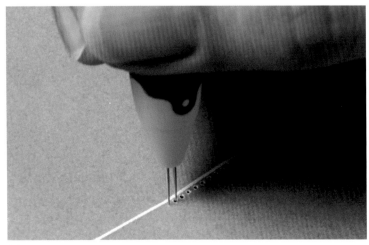

Start by placing your parchment on your embossing mat. On the back of your parchment, emboss a straight line using a Groovi plate or a ruler and the number 1 Clarity (1mm Pergamano) or number 2 Clarity (1.5mm-Pergama embossing tool. Turn your parchment over and place your perforating mat (this is the right side of your wo

Now use the repeated insertions technique as follow position the first 2-needle perforations close to the outside edge of your embossed line (as close as you can without actually perforating the line, as this will make your work look untidy). Now, to keep the distance between the perforations equal throughout, insert one needle in the last hole of this first 2-needle perforation. This will advance your perforations around your embossed line by one hole at a time. By maintaining even perforations in this way, your work will be much neater. When you have finished perforating, you can start cutting your picot edge.
N.B. On the 2-needle tool, you will find that one of the needles is slightly longer than the other. It's easier to use this needle when relocating the tool into the last hole made.

16

Photocopy this pattern to try the sampler for yourself.

Sampler Pattern: 2-Needle & 3-Needle Tools

2-needle and 3-needle perforating tools

Star tools 2mm, wheel

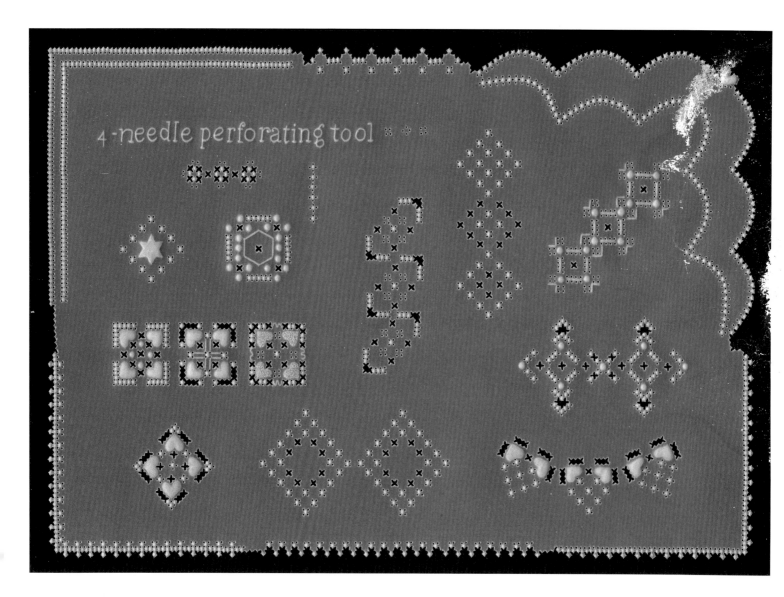

4-Needle Tool PER-TO-70036-XX (10251)

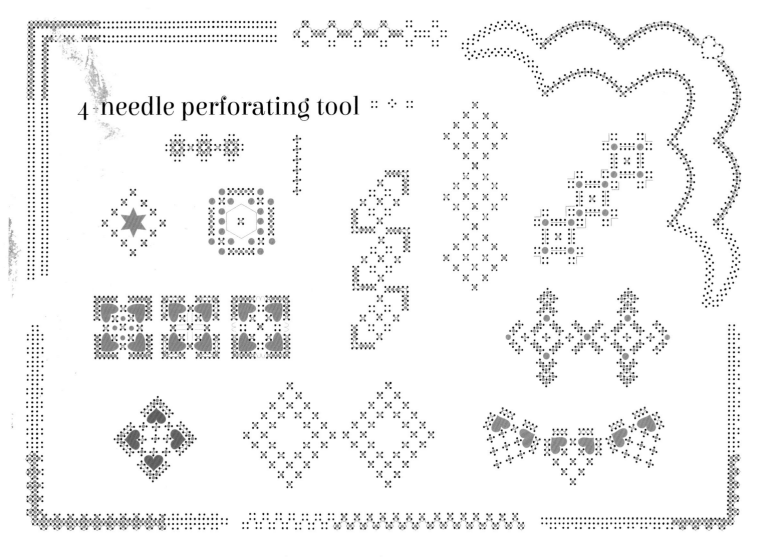

4-needle perforating tool

● Perforate ● Emboss ⌄ Cut

4-Needle Tool

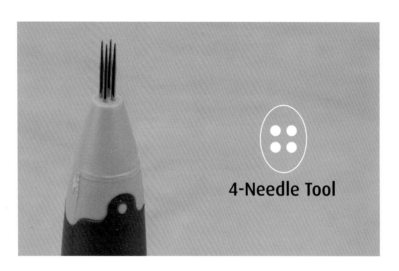

4-Needle Tool

The most versatile of all the tools.
The four needle tool is the most popular multi-needle tool, and it's also the most frequently used. When cut correctly, it forms a neat cross.

Using clever configurations and perforating with the four needle tool, you can produce the most exquisite lacework.

Dots and shapes can be embossed between the four needle perforations. Also, instead of cutting the perforations out, you can very carefully emboss a dot in the centre of eac¹ four needle perforation. Use the 1mm ball tool for this.

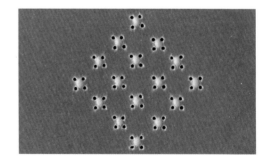

The four needle tool can also be used to perforate on the fine straight grid. Similarly, the BOLD four needle tool works with the bold straight grid.

There are far too many ways to use the four needle tool to list here; it's quite simply the best tool for creating patterns. Use your imagination, or have a look around for patterns using this tool. The possibilities are endless!

Photocopy this pattern
to try the sampler for
yourself.

**Sampler Pattern:
4-Needle Tool**

4-needle perforating tool

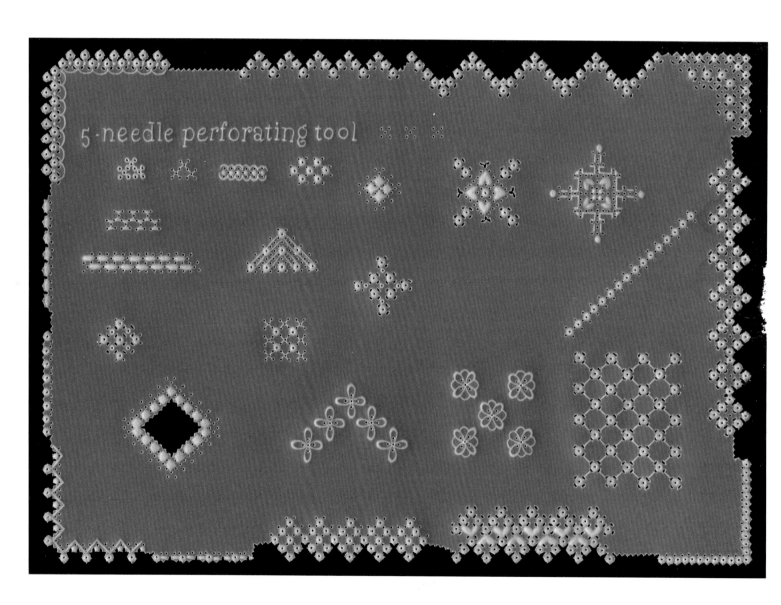

5-needle perforating tool

5-Needle Tool PER-TO-70019-XX (10212)

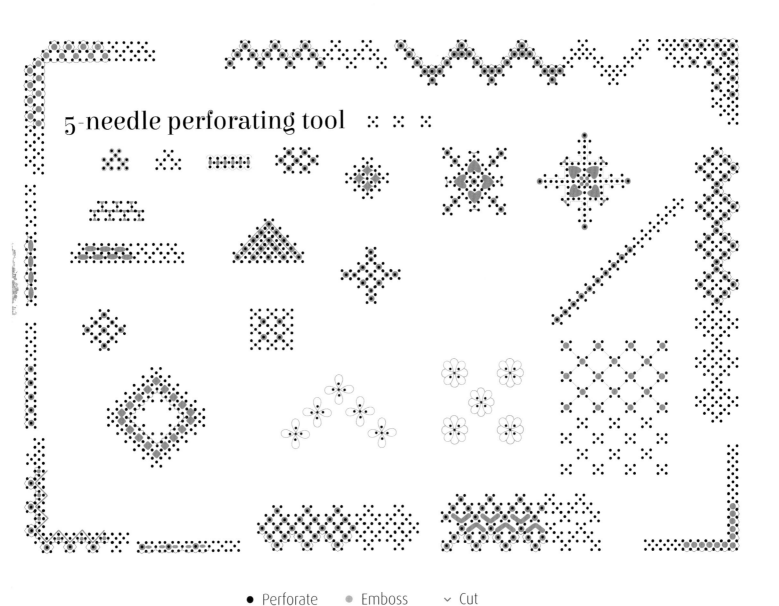

5-needle perforating tool

● Perforate ● Emboss ⌄ Cut

5-Needle Tool

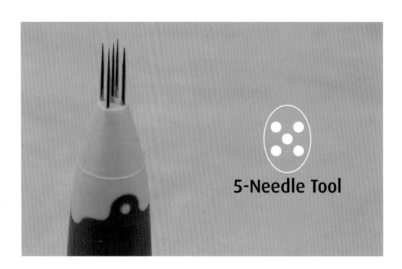

5-Needle Tool

5-needle tool with a twist

This is a slightly different technique, but it gives a lovely effect which you can see on the example sheet. With the 5-needle tool, perforate shallow as normal (1). Remove the parchment paper from the pattern. Now place your piece face down on the embossing mat and emboss a generous circle around the middle perforation, using the 1.5mm embossing tool (2). It doesn't matter if you flatten the perforation at this point. Now re-perforate with the 5-needle tool. Notice on the sample sheet that some of the 5-needle tool perforations have elongated holes. To achieve this effect, when you perforate deeply, twist the tool slightly (in a circular motion) to the left and then to the right so that the holes elongate slightly (3). Be careful not to twist too much, or the holes will meet and the middle will fall out! Try to twist each 5-needle tool the same amount, so that they appear uniform. You can try different combinations of twisting see (4). This is a straight row of 5-needle perforations, with every other 5-needle centre embossed. In the top example, every alternate embossed perforation has been twisted. In the bottom example, it's the opposite; each alternate un-embossed perforation has been twisted. See the different pattern it produces from the same perforation pattern. Magic!

Also, you can also employ this twisting technique with a Five in a Circle tool.

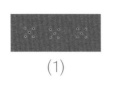

(1)

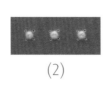

(2)

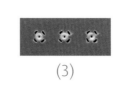

(3)

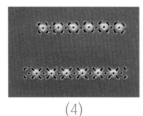

(4)

Photocopy this pattern to try the sampler for yourself.

**Sampler Pattern:
5-Needle Tool**

5-needle perforating tool

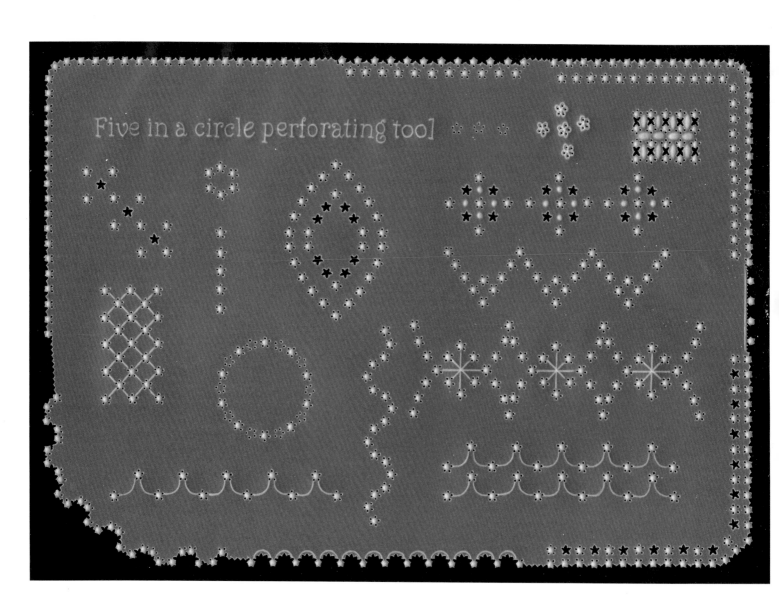

Five in a circle perforating tool

5 in a Circle Tool PER-TO-70025-XX (10223)

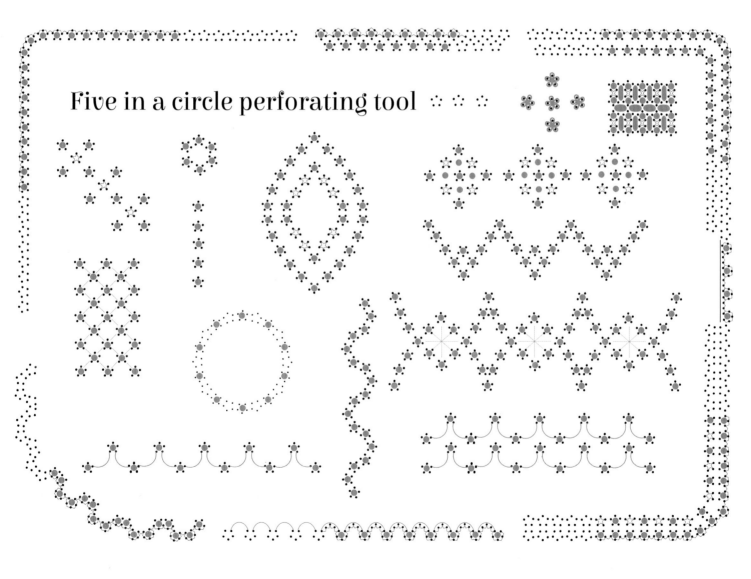

Five in a circle perforating tool

● Perforate ● Emboss ⌄ Cut

5 in a Circle Tool

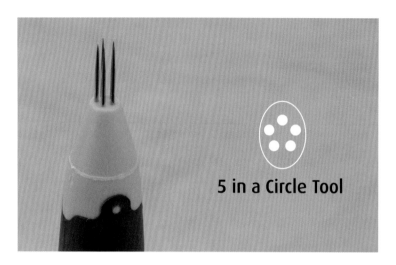

5 in a Circle Tool

5 in a Circle Tool, brill as a fill!

The 5 in a circle tool has more uses than you can imagine. It's a great tool for filling large areas with randomly spaced perforations.

The best way to show off this tool is to fill the centre with a lovely white embossed dot.

It can also be used to create beautiful combinations and decorative borders. The five in a circle looks particularly lovely when used to decorate a scalloped edge.

You can also perforate with a twist, as shown previously for the five needle tool. Although, be extra careful when doing this, as the gap between the needles is smaller on this tool. And you may tear a hole!

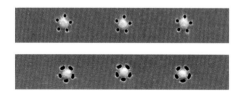

Photocopy this pattern
to try the sampler for
yourself.

**Sampler Pattern:
5 in a Circle Tool**

Five in a circle perforating tool

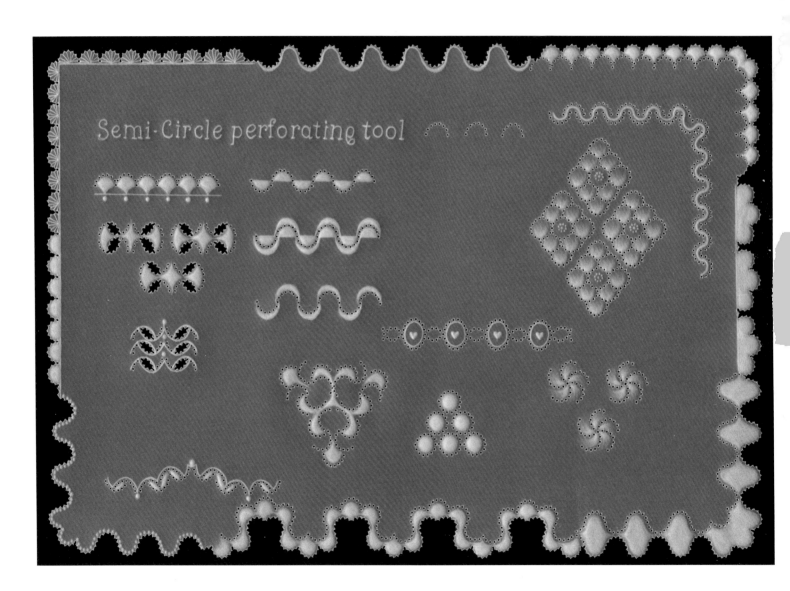

Semi-Circle perforating tool

Semi-Circle Tool PER-TO-70017-XX (10209)

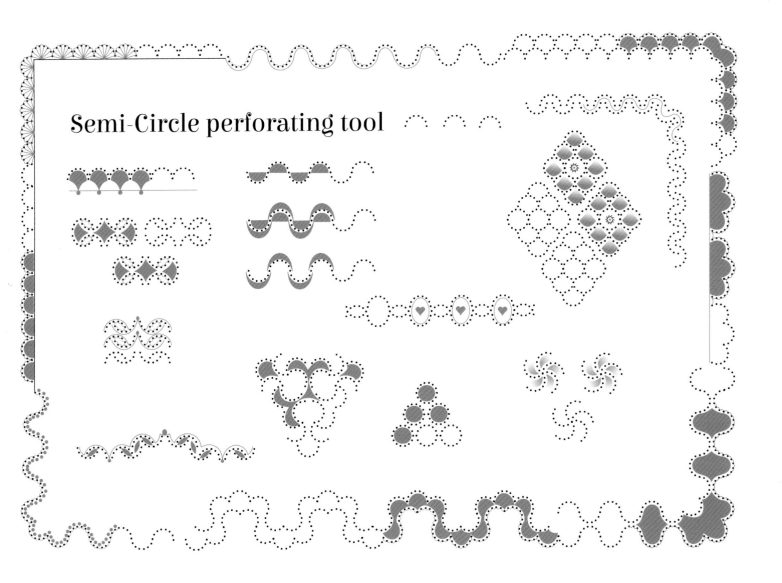

Semi-Circle perforating tool

● Perforate ● Emboss ⌄ Cut

Semi-Circle Tool

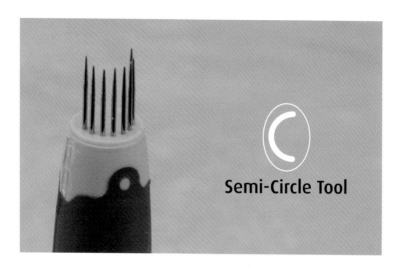

Semi-Circle Tool

Something to take the edge off!

The Semi-Circle Tool is one of the oldest and much loved tools. It is popular because it makes a great edging tool. When using this tool on the edge of a project, you can use the repeat insertion technique i.e. put the first needle of the tool into the last hole of your previous perforations.

Alternatively, you can leave a slight gap, about the width of a two needle tool. If you are going to cut out around these perforations, you might prefer to have the extra space in between to make it easier for you to cut where the semi-circles meet.

The Semi-Circle Mini Tool will fit neatly inside the Semi-Circle Tool.

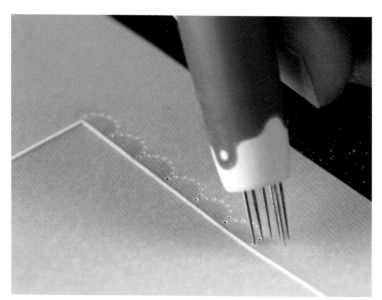

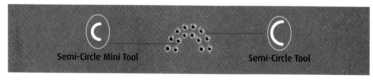

Semi-Circle Mini Tool   Semi-Circle Tool

You will notice the first and last needles of the tool are longer than the others. This is help with the repeat insertion technique.

Photocopy this pattern
to try the sampler for
yourself.

Sampler Pattern: Semi-Circle Tool

Semi-Circle perforating tool

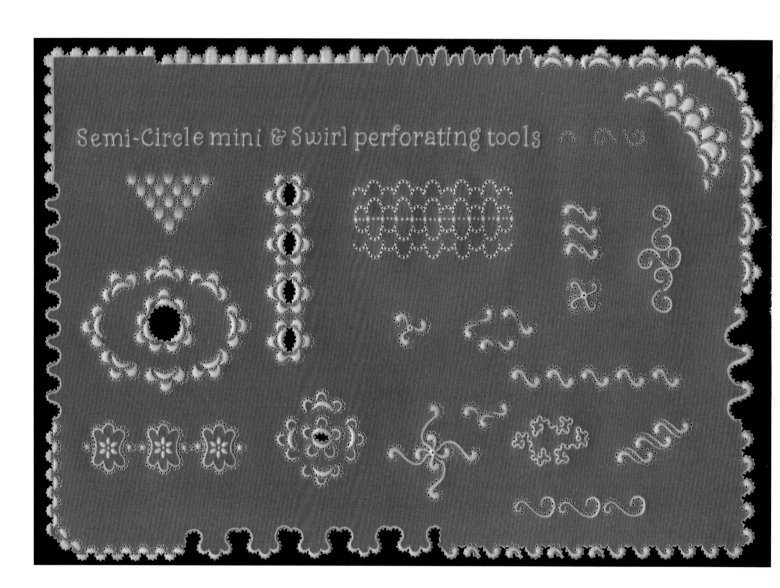

Semi-Circle Mini Tool PER-TO-70034-XX (10237)

Swirl Tool PER-TO-70032-XX (10235)

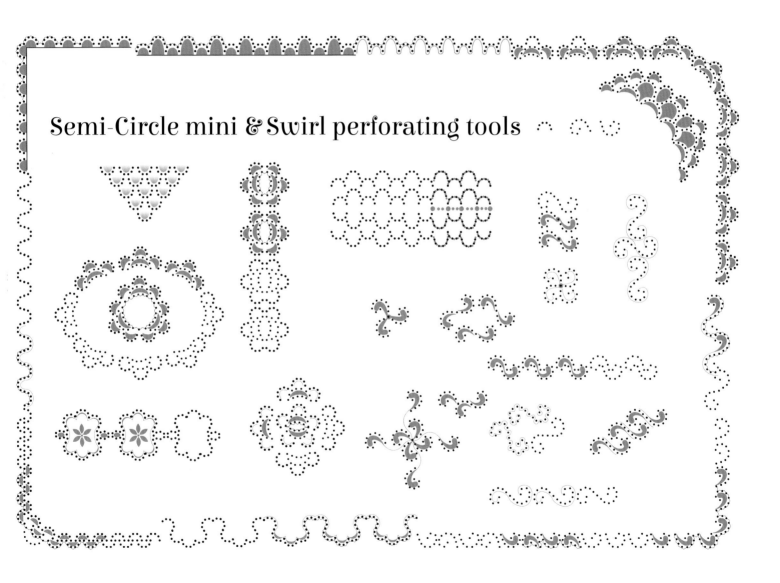

Semi-Circle mini & Swirl perforating tools

● Perforate   ● Emboss   ⌄ Cut

Semi-Circle Mini & Swirl Tools

Semi-Circle Mini Tool

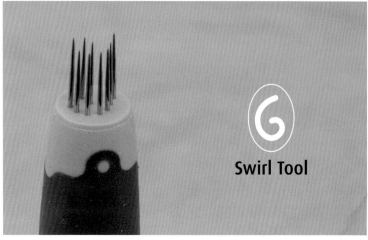

Swirl Tool

A Neat Little Tool

The Semi-Circle Mini Tool has similar uses to the Semi-Circle tool. A beautiful edge can be created by using these tools alternately.

On the pattern sheet opposite, you will see the occasional use of the moon tool to facilitate pattern creation. If you do not have the moon tool, simply use the 1-Needle Tool to create these perforations.

Give us a twirl!

This is a relatively new decorative needle tool, and is really useful for creating scrolls and wave patterns within your design.

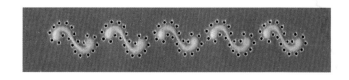

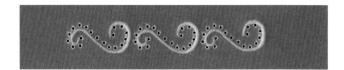

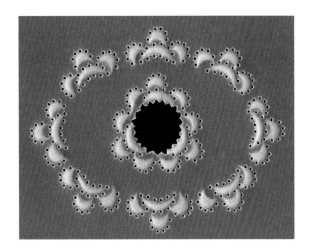

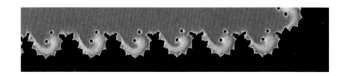

It looks particularly good when perforated back-to-back to create a beautiful insert or border.

Photocopy this pattern
to try the sampler for
yourself.

**Sampler Pattern:
Semi-Circle Mini & Swirl Tools**

Semi-Circle mini & Swirl perforating tools

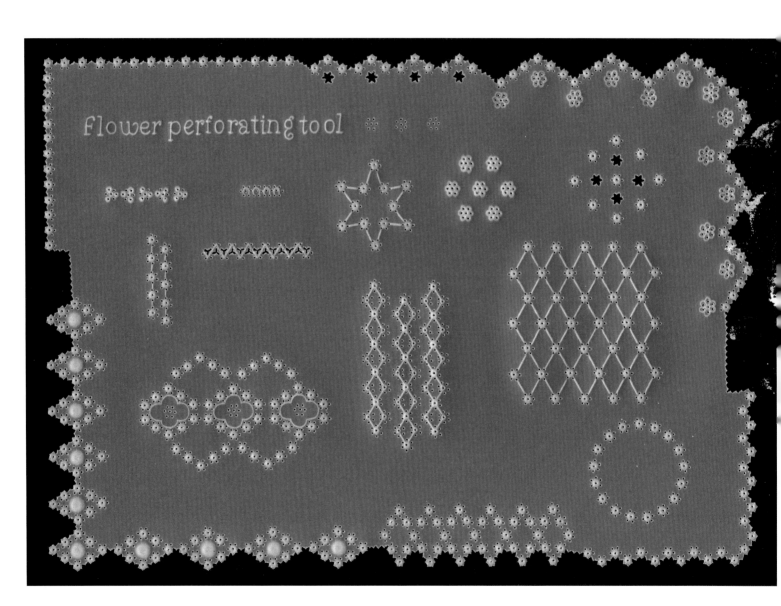

flower perforating tool

Flower Tool PER-TO-70018-XX (10211)

Flower perforating tool

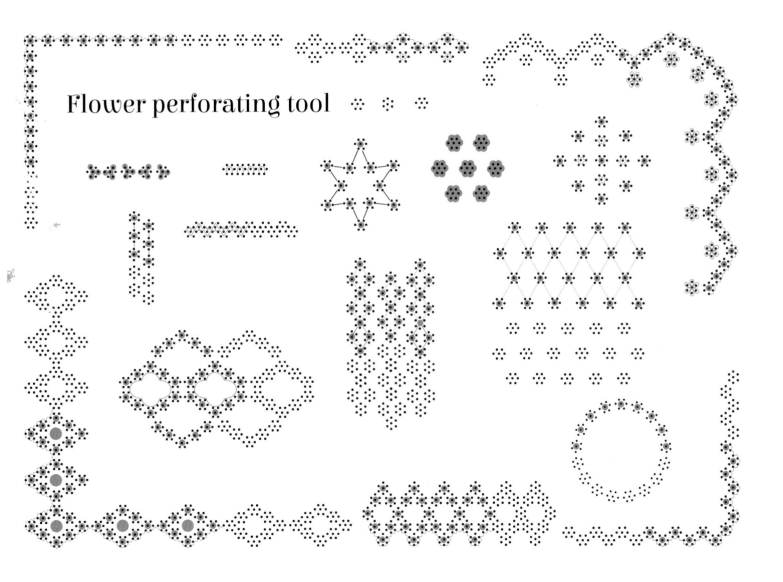

● Perforate   ● Emboss   ⌄ Cut

39

Flower Tool

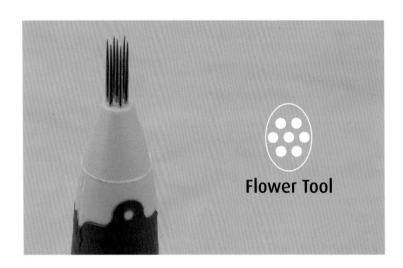

Flower Tool

Say it with flowers...

The Flower tool serves as another beautiful border or infill tool. With this tool, try embossing a circle around each perforation using the 1mm ball tool. Then re-perforate to widen the holes, this time with the one needle tool for accuracy. This also gives a neater finish.

This creates the prettiest flower, that really stands out!

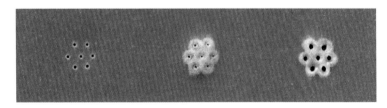

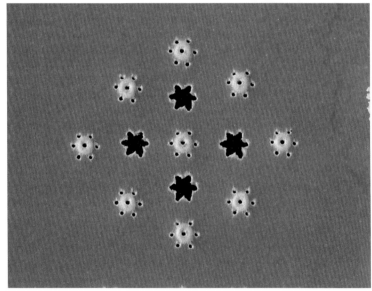

Instead of embossing, why not try cutting out within the perforations to produce a star shape. This is great for Christmas cards.

Photocopy this pattern
to try the sampler for
yourself.

**Sampler Pattern:
Flower Tool**

Flower perforating tool

Perfect Your Cutting

In parchment craft, good cutting is all about snipping the connections between each perforation, to ensure a neat and even picot point. This takes a little patience and practice, and a good technique from the onset is important. You will also need to make sure that you can see clearly. Make sure your eyes, glasses and/or magnifier are up to the job and that you are working in good light. You will not get a good result or be able to perfect your technique if you can't see what you are doing! Make sure you can see the tips of your scissors going into the perforated holes in the parchment. Do not guess this, it won't work!

1. Position your parchment on your cutting mat, right side uppermost. During cutting, you need to make sure that the waste parchment i.e. the parchment that you are cutting away, is always positioned underneath the blades of your scissors when the points are inserted in to the perforations. Diagram A illustrates the difference between the picot edge and the edge that is left on the waste parchment.

Always aim to keep the scissors at a right angle to the line you are cutting. Whether you have a straight line, a curved line, or need to turn a corner, it is very important to turn the parchment and not your scissors! Always keep your hand and scissors in the same position, this will ensure you have neat, evenly formed points (see Diagram B1 and B2).

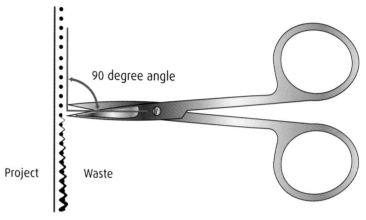

Diagram B1

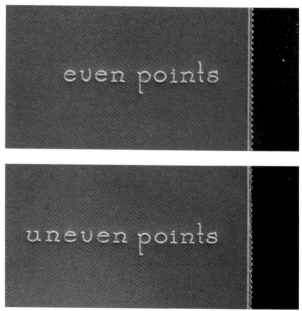

Diagram B2

Diagram A

Perfect Your Cutting

Cutting Method 1 (fork)

2.   Hold the scissors with the curved end pointing downwards, like a fork. Put your right forefinger down into the left aperture of the scissors and your middle finger down into the right aperture. Brace your thumb against the outside of the left aperture. If you are left-handed, place the forefinger of your left hand down into the right aperture and the middle finger down into the left aperture. Holding your scissors in this way may feel a little alien at first, but this is the conventional and most used way. There are numerous other ways, so try and find the most comfortable way that suits you. You could also try using cutting method 2 (my preferred method).

3.   Now insert the points of the scissors (not too deeply) into the two perforations that are nearest to you.

4.   Next, drop the scissors down toward the paper as much as possible, without removing the tips from the perforations. The scissors should be almost parallel to the paper.

5.   Start the cutting motion and cut the connection between the perforations, twisting your hand and the scissors very slightly towards you as you snip. You will hear a snapping noise each time you cut. A small point will be created between the perforations after each cut. Now move upwards along the line of perforations, cutting each connection as you go. Use this technique when cutting out around and within lacework.

The fork method for holding the scissors when cutting parchment.

Perfect Your Cutting

Cutting Method 2 (spoon)

Follow step 1, then hold the scissors with the curved end pointing upwards, like a spoon. Put the thumb of your right hand up into the left aperture of the scissors and your first finger up into the right aperture.

This might feel more comfortable than the FORK method. If you are left handed, this way may be easier too.

Finally return to steps 3 – 5 of the fork method.

The spoon method for holding the scissors when cutting parchment.

Still can't get it right?

Slowly does it, with lots of practice!
When you first learn to cut, it's best to almost cut in slow motion. Program yourself to cut slowly, and then when you have perfected your technique, and it is imprinted in your brain, you can speed up. Try the following method.
Follow steps 1 – 4 above.

5.	At this point, instead of cutting the parchment, close the scissors slowly, as if to pinch, until you can actually see the point forming (see Diagram C). Then and only then, do you actually snip and twist to execute the cut.

This is more time consuming, but it will pay off in the end. Once you have the correct technique for you, then you can speed up.

When you can cut along a straight line, practice cutting around a curved or wavy line, always remembering to turn your parchment whilst keeping your scissors in the same position. You can also perforate and cut out within a shape, or several shapes, to produce beautiful patterns and combinations.

Pinch slowly to form the points.

Diagram C

Cutting A Cross

You will need: parchment paper, perforating mat, cutting mat, 4 needle perforating tool and parchment scissors.

1.   Position the parchment, right side up, onto the perforating mat.

2.   Perforate deeply with the 4-needle tool.

3.   Place the points of your scissors into perforations 1 and 2. Lower your scissors so that they are almost parallel to the parchment paper. Now make your first cut, tilting your scissors very slightly towards you as you do so. This should form a neat point. Diagram D

4.   Turn your parchment a quarter turn to the left, so that holes 2 and 3 are uppermost, and repeat the cutting process. Diagram E

5.   Turn the parchment a quarter turn to the left again, so that holes 3 and 4 are uppermost and cut as before. Diagram F

6.   Turn the parchment for the last time so that holes 4 and 1 are now uppermost, and make your final cut. At this stage, the centre should fall out, leaving a neat cross shape. Diagram G

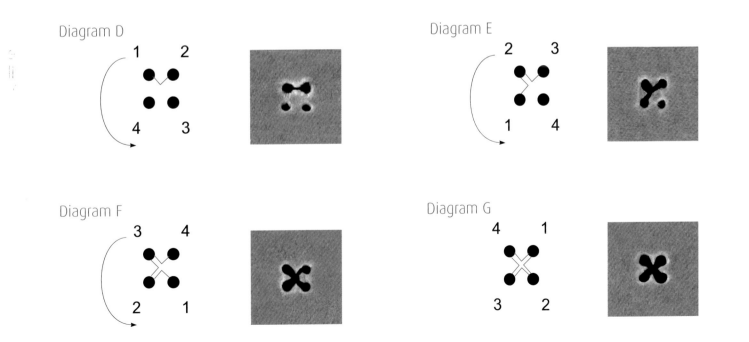

Diagram D

Diagram E

Diagram F

Diagram G

From Crosses To Lace

When you have mastered cutting out a cross, the world is your oyster with regards to lacework and gridwork. A lot of the beautiful lacework we see today is a combination of embossing and intricate cutwork, which is just multiple combinations of perforated and cut crosses.

Diagram H1 illustrates a simple 4-needle combination. This can be achieved by printing out the pattern and placing the parchment on top. Then perforate, using the 4-needle tool, through the parchment and the pattern to ensure correct positioning.

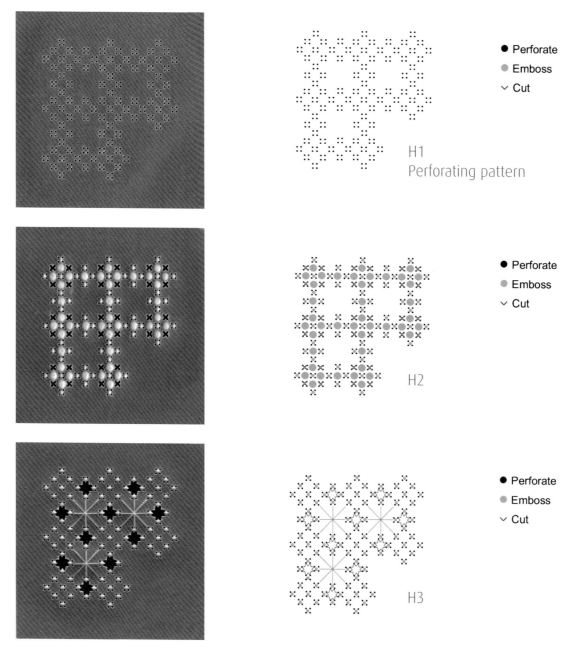

H1
Perforating pattern

● Perforate
◉ Emboss
∨ Cut

H2

● Perforate
◉ Emboss
∨ Cut

H3

● Perforate
◉ Emboss
∨ Cut

From Crosses To Lace

Lace H2, H3, H4, and H5 have all been made from the same pattern. See how different they can look by embossing different areas and cutting out different 4 – needle combinations! Note how they become increasingly more complicated. Most patterns can be adapted to accommodate your skill level.

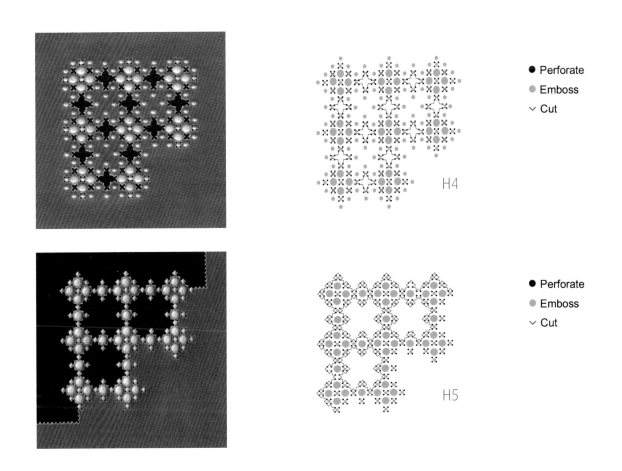

● Perforate
● Emboss
⌄ Cut

H4

● Perforate
● Emboss
⌄ Cut

H5

Top Tip

When you are cutting between some perforations, depending on what tool or combination you have used, you may find that some gaps are a little wider than others. Cut these perforations first, then go back and cut the narrower ones. You might find your lacework will be a lot neater this way.

Perforating Tools Used

2 Needle
PER-TO-70037-XX
(10261)

3 Needle
PER-TO-70038-XX
(10281)

2mm Star
PER-TO-70006-XX
(10211)

Pattern Map

Home Is Where You Park It

Project Difficulty 2 - Intermediate

Ingredients

Motor Vehicle plate
Mini plate mate
Mini circle plate
Nested scallops rectangles
Blendable pencils
Dorso oil or other blending solution
Star 2mm
2-needle perforating tool
3-needle perforating tool
Embossing tools
Perga colours exclusive
Flower brad x 1
Clarity 'Brighton Rock' Designer Paper Pad

To Make

1 Emboss camper van and circle (3rd circle in) on a small piece of parchment. Decorate and emboss van with flowers, hearts and scallops. Dorso with colours of your choice. Perforate around with 2-needle tool and cut out.

50

2 On another piece of parchment, draw in a wavy line close to the bottom using a white pencil. Using the mini plate mate alphabet, emboss "Home is where you park it" or "Life is a journey". Rub out pencil line and emboss letters. Emboss a rectangle around (2nd rectangle in).

3 Dorso green below script. Above script, dorso round bubbles using the same colourway as the van. Emboss flowers on grass using Star 2mm. Emboss a dot in each centre with the 0.5mm tool.

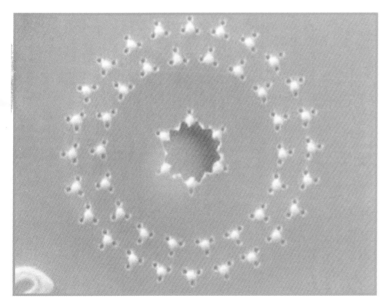

4 Using the circular 3 needle pattern, position underneath the round bubbles and perforate shallow using the 3-needle tool. Emboss dots in middle with 1mm tool, and then re-perforate. Cut out centre part, following pattern.

5 On the back, colour between double outline of border using felt tip pen. Perforate with 2-needle tool around the outer border and cut out. Fold at top and add an insert of white card and Candy Shop paper. Attach camper van circle using a brad.

Colourful Balloons

Perforating Tools Used

5 in a Circle
PER-TO-70025-XX
(10223)

Semi-Circle
PER-TO-70017-XX
(10209)

4-Needle
PER-TO-70036-XX
(10251)

Pattern Map

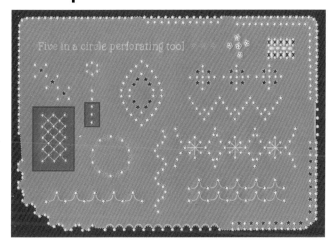

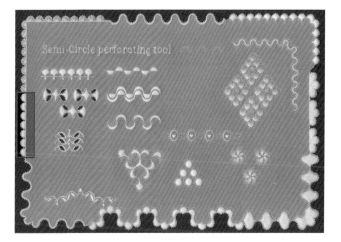

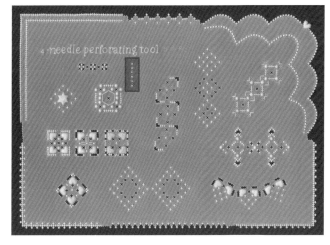

Colourful Balloons

Project Difficulty 1 - Easiest

Ingredients

Hot Air Balloon plate
Houses and Geese plate
Mini plate mate
Mini nested squares plate
Jayne's small alphabet frame plate
Blendable pencils
Dorso oil or other blending solution
4-needle perforating tool
Five in a Circle perforating tool
Semi-circle perforating tool
Embossing tools
Shader embossing tool
Distress markers
Pergamano Brads x 4
Clarity 'Northern Lights' Designer Paper Pad

To Make

1 Emboss a square frame using the mini nested squares (largest square). Use the same plate to make an outer square by carefully extending the lines.

2 Using Jayne's frame plate (sixth square in), emboss the larger square and then emboss another square outside this by extending the lines a little.

3 Emboss the balloons, clouds, trees and birds, following the coloured picture.

4 Colour the balloons and trees using the Distress markers. Dorso the sky using blue, pink and yellow blendable pencils, blended with Dorso oil.

5 Perforate shallow using the 4-needle and Five in a Circle tools within the balloons, and using the semi-circle tool around the outer border. Follow the pattern indicated.

6 Emboss the shapes within the needle tool perforations. Re-perforate with the needle tools. Cut out around the semi-circle border.

7 Mat and layer using the Northern Lights designer paper and white card.

Perforating Tools Used

Flower
PER-TO-70018-XX
(10211)

Pattern Map

Happy New Home

Project Difficulty 2 - Intermediate

Ingredients

Village A5 plate
Family and Blessings word chain border plate
Nested Squares Extension and Small Alphabet Frame plate
Mountains and Hills Groovi plate A5
Nested Tags Groovi plate A5
Blendable pencils
Dorso oil or other blending solution
Flower perforating tool
Embossing tools
Pergamano Brads x 4
Teal Groovi parchment
3mm crystal gems
Distress markers
Perga glue
Ribbon

To Make

1 Using the indicated pattern on page 61, shallow perforate the frame with the flower tool.

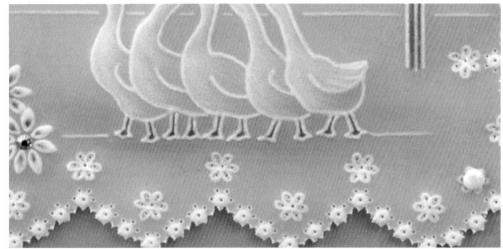

2 Using embossing tool 1.5mm, emboss the dots within the perforations, as indicated on the pattern. With a 0.5mm tool, emboss the flower shapes around the remaining perforations, as indicated.

3 Perforate deep with the flower tool, and then cut out around the outer perforations.

4 Within this frame, emboss the geese, sign post, daisies and houses from the Village plate. Emboss "New Home" following the curve of the row of houses. Add some embossed landscape lines from the Mountains and Hills plate. With 4.5mm tool emboss the geese.

5 On the back, use coloured pencils and dorso oil to colour the grass, road and sky. Use Distress markers to colour the houses, flowers and signpost.

6 Mat and layer using the teal parchment and white card.

7 Make a layered tag using the nested tags, and add a sentiment of your choice. Stick onto the card, add a bow and some gems.

Photocopy this pattern to
try the card for yourself.

Top

Happy New Home Card Pattern

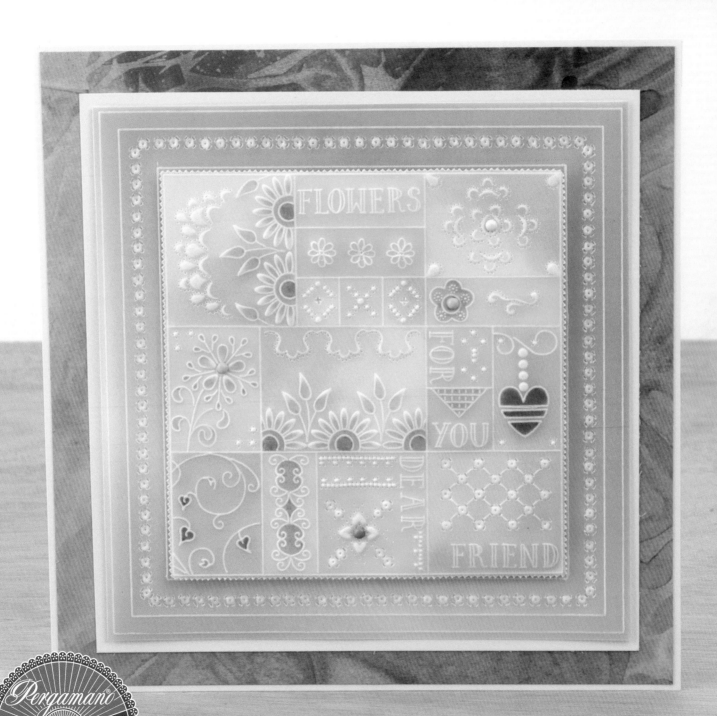

Perforating Tools Used

 **2 Needle**
PER-TO-70037-XX
(10261)
 4-Needle
PER-TO-70036-XX
(10251)
 5-Needle
PER-TO-70019-XX
(10212)
 **Semi-Circle**
PER-TO-70017-XX
(10209)

 Semi-Circle Mini
PER-TO-70034-XX
(10237)
 Swirl
PER-TO-70032-XX
(10235)
 2mm Star
PER-TO-70006-XX
(10211)
 **Moon**
PER-TO-70031-XX
(10232)

Pattern Map

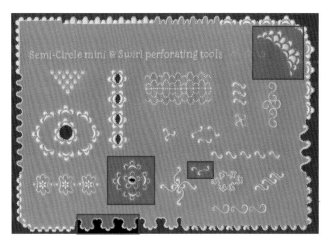

Ingredients

Mistletoe and Wreath accessories plate
Nested Squares Extension and Small Alphabet Frame plate
Alphabet Picture Frame square plate
Tina's Henna Corners 1 plate
Tina's Floral Swirls & Corners 1 plate
Tina's Christmas Corners 2 plate
Nested Squares or Rectangles plate
Any small alphabet plate
Oooh-La-La Bra plate
2-needle perforating tool
4-needle perforating tool
5-needle perforating tool
Semi-circle perforating tool
Semi-circle Mini perforating tool
Moon perforating tool
Swirl perforating tool
Star 2mm
Various embossing ball tools
Pergamano Brads x 4
Pergamano Orange parchment paper
Perga Colours Exclusive (PCE) Pens
Coloured pencils
Dorso oil
Clarity 'Northern Lights' Designer Paper

Needle Sampler

Project Difficulty 3 - Advanced

To Make

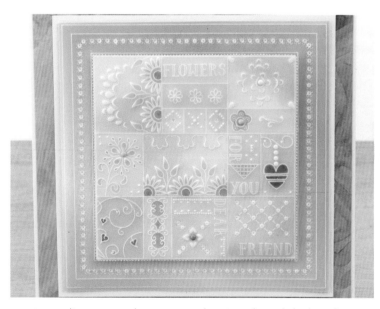

1   On ordinary parchment, and using the Alphabet frame, emboss the inner square frame. Using the Nested Squares or Rectangles, add the dividing lines. You can divide the square up in different combinations, and decorate as you wish; no two cards need ever be the same! Have fun playing with this concept! On orange parchment paper and using the Nested Squares Extension and Small Alphabet Frame, emboss a double frame to measure 14cm x 14cm.

2   Use any small alphabet Groovi Plate to add your chosen greetings or sentiments in different boxes. Then decorate using the plates listed in the ingredients, or any other plates of your choice. Make sure to leave some spaces for the needle tool work.

3   Using the PCE pens, colour in the small areas with your chosen colours. Dorso the larger areas.

4   Using your chosen needle tools and patterns provided, perforate shallow to fill in the empty spaces. Also using the 5-needle tool, perforate around the inner part of the frame on the orange parchment.

5   Emboss within these perforations, following the embossing patterns. Emboss using the star 2mm. Emboss to create shading on the flowers etc.

6   Perforate deep, using the appropriate tools. Perforate the 5-needle tool with a twist. Using the 2-needle tool, perforate and then cut out around the sampler square. Cut out around the orange square, using a craft knife.

7   Now mat and layer the two parchment pieces with white card and the Designer Paper, using the brads to secure.

Photocopy this pattern to
try the card for yourself.

Top

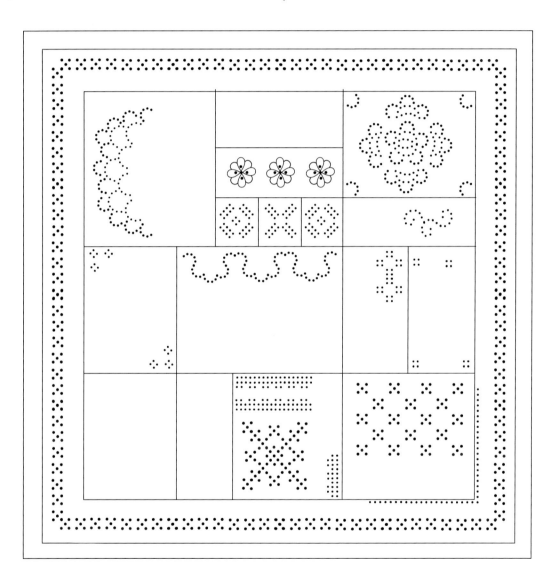

Needle Sampler Card Pattern

Perforating Tools Used

2 Needle
PER-TO-70037-XX
(10261)

5 Needle
PER-TO-70019-XX
(10212)

Pattern Map

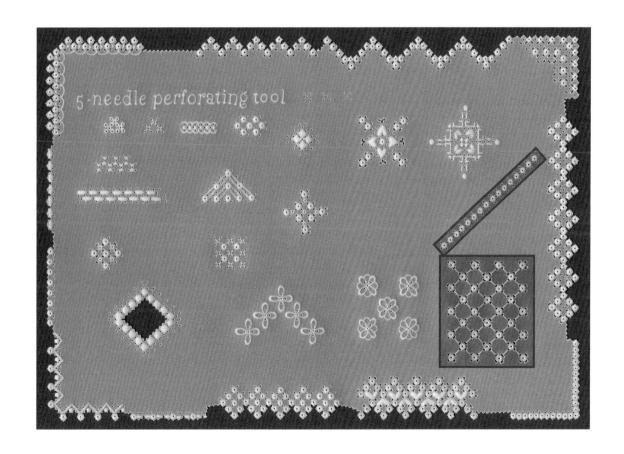

Noel

Project Difficulty 1 - Easiest

To Make

Ingredients

Twiggy Wreath plate A4
Ribbons and Bows plate A5
Nested Octagons plate A5
Christmas Word Chains border plate
2-needle perforating tool
5-needle perforating tool
Various ball embossing tools
Pergamano Brads x 4
Groovi light ivory parchment paper
Mica Gold paste
Distress Markers
Sticky ink
Pergamano mapping pen
Pergamano glitters

1   On ivory parchment, emboss the bow first, and then emboss the twiggy wreath behind the bow. Emboss "Noel" in the centre. Position on the octagon plate and emboss the second and third largest octagons, avoiding the bow. Reposition, rotating the parchment slightly so that the points of the octagon appear half way along the straight edge (see picture above). Emboss these angles. On the back of the parchment and using a damp brush, colour lightly between the double outlines, with ink taken from a matching Distress Marker. Also colour behind the bow and greeting to lightly create shading. Use pencils if not confident with a brush.

2   Cut a square of ivory parchment to measure 14.5cm x 16cm. Perforate shallow with the 5-needle tool in each corner of the square (see indicated pattern) and also between the double outlines of the octagon. Emboss a dot within each 5-needle perforation using the 1.5mm ball tool. Then perforate deep with a twist (see instructions for 5-Needle Tool Page 24).

3   Using a 4.5mm and 3mm ball tool, emboss the letters.

4   Mix the gold mica paste with some water to create an inky consistency. Trace gold lines along the edge of the twigs, down one side of each letter and dots within the edge of the border on the bow. Using neat paste and a 3mm ball tool, create dip dots for berries. Allow to dry completely. Emboss the dip dots with a 1.5mm ball tool.

5   With the 2-needle tool, perforate within each corner and around the outside of the octagonal frame. Cut out around these perforations.

6   Now mat and layer the two parchment pieces with white and gold card, held in place with brads.

7   Add sticky ink and glitter.

Photocopy this pattern to
try the card for yourself.

Top

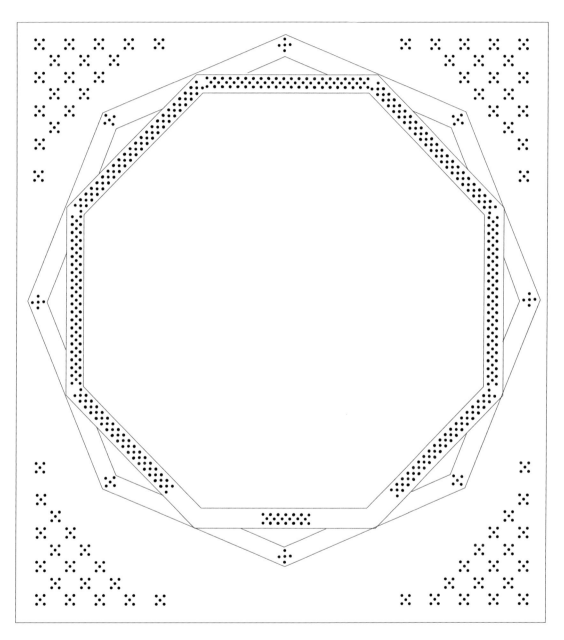

Noel Card Pattern

Perforating Tools Used

2 Needle
PER-TO-70037-XX
(10261)

5 in a Circle
PER-TO-70025-XX
(10223)

Pattern Map

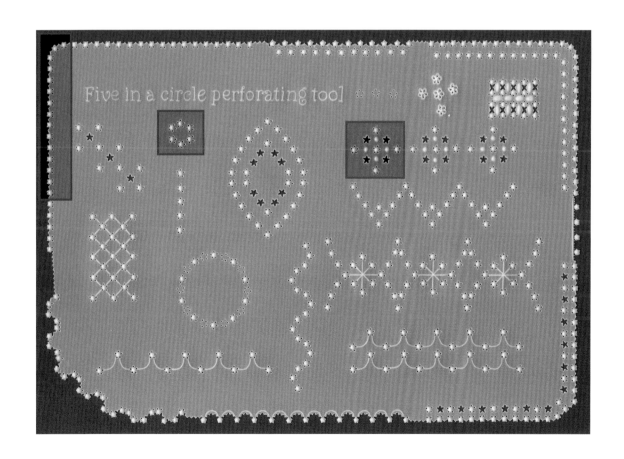

Teddy Bib

Project Difficulty 2 - Intermediate

Ingredients

Jayne's Christmas Eve plate
Nested Squares Extension and Small Alphabet Frame plate
Nested Scallops Circles plate A5 square
Oooh-La-La Bra plate A4 square
Blendable pencils
Dorso oil or other blending solution
2-needle perforating tool
Five in a circle perforating tool
Various ball embossing tools
Pergamano Brads x 4
Groovi shades of pink parchment paper
Perga glue
Pink organza ribbon

To Make

1   Emboss the teddy on ordinary parchment paper. Emboss a heart in his paw. Decide how many blocks you need for the name, centre and emboss. Using the alphabet frame, emboss the name within the blocks.

2 Using the nested scalloped circles, emboss a small double outline circle, avoiding the teddy. Now emboss the second largest double outline (offset) to form the bib shape (see colour picture).

3 On the back of the parchment, use coloured pencils to colour the bear, bow, heart and blocks. Blend if you wish. Also colour between the double outlines of the circles.

4 Perforate shallow with the five in a circle perforating tool, around the inner and outer circle and within the bib (following the indicated pattern). Emboss a dot within each needle tool perforation, and then perforate deep.

5 Perforate around the upper part of the teddy and heart using the 2-needle tool. Cut out around the inner and outer circles to form the bib.

6 On the dark pink parchment, emboss another bib using larger circles. Also emboss the scallops and dots on the outer edge. Perforate around with the 2-needle tool and cut out.

7 Now mat and layer the two parts of the bib, along with various squares of light and dark pink parchment and layers of white card. Add a bow.

77

Perforating Tools Used

2 Needle
PER-TO-70037-XX
(10261)

4-Needle
PER-TO-70036-XX
(10251)

5 in a Circle
PER-TO-70025-XX
(10223)

Pattern Map

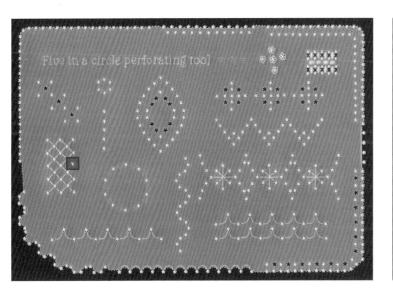

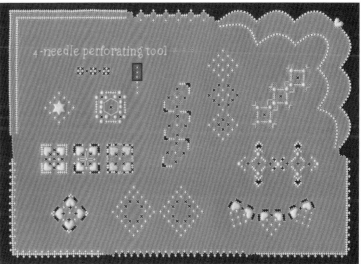

Ingredients

Tina's 3D Flowers and Butterflies plate A4
Nested Squares Extension and Small Alphabet Frame plate
Nested Circles plate A5
Small Nested Circles baby plate A6
Ribbon and Hearts border plate
Blendable pencils
Dorso oil or other blending solution
2-needle perforating tool
4-needle perforating tool
Five in a circle perforating tool
Wheel embossing tool
Various ball embossing tools
Pergamano Brads x 2
Pergamano lime green and pink parchment paper
Perga glue
Sticky ink
Pergamano mapping pen
Pergamano glitters
Perga colours exclusive

Hello Flower

Project Difficulty 2 - Intermediate

To Make

1   Emboss 3D flowers, leaves and butterflies of your choice. Colour them on the back with coloured pencils blended with Dorso oil.

2   Decorate the flowers in the following way: perforate shallow with either the 4-needle or five in a circle tool. Emboss a dot within, using the appropriate embossing tool, and then perforate deep. Alternatively, you can achieve a linen look by running the wheel tool backwards and forwards over the back of your work, going in both directions. Don't worry about going over the lines, as you will be cutting out the flower.

3   On a spare piece of parchment, emboss "HELLO Flower" and create circles around using the circle plate of your choice. Colour on the back as before and add some five in a circle perforations. Also create a larger circle decorated with the cheque effect, as described in step 4.

4   Create a band of parchment 7cm x 18cm, enough to wrap around your card. The check edges are created by embossing double rows of straight lines, in both directions. Use Dorso to colour the back of the strip. Colour the space within the sets of lines using felt tip pens.

5   Perforate around all the 3D elements using the 2-needle tool and then cut out.

6   Now mat and layer using the pink and green parchment and layers of white card. Wrap around the wide band and secure at the back. Add the decorative circles using brads, and stick on the 3D flowers, leaves and butterflies with Perga glue. Add glue and glitter.

Perforating Tools Used

2 Needle
PER-TO-70037-XX
(10261)

4-Needle
PER-TO-70036-XX
(10251)

Pattern Map

Ingredients

Nested rectangles plate plate
Gentleman's bicycle plate
Floral circle plate
Postage plate
Jayne's large and small alphabet frame plates
2-needle perforating tool
4-needle perforating tool
Embossing tools
Wheel embossing tool
Pergamano Hydrangea purple parchment paper
Blendable pencils
Dorso oil or other blending solution
Distress Markers
Glitter brads x 5
Clarity 'Sweet Dreams' Designer Paper Pad

May Life Be A Beautiful Ride

Project Difficulty 3 - Advanced

To Make

1   Firstly, emboss a small spray of flower for the front basket (see picture). Emboss the bicycle as a single seater, taking care to avoid the flowers. Now emboss the flowers cascading from the back, and emboss in another basket within the space between flowers and bicycle. Emboss a rectangle around the subject, and add a stamp edge. Colour on the back with Distress Markers. Cut out with a straight edge.

2 Place rectangle on another piece of parchment and draw in a swirl using a white pencil. Using the floral plate, emboss flowers randomly to cascade along this swirl. Add some flourishes with the embossing wheel. Rub out pencil mark. Colour on the back with Distress Markers, fading the colouring as you go around, eventually ending with white embossed flowers at the end.

3 With a white pencil, draw a small curve again, along which you can emboss the words "MAY LIFE". Then emboss "Be a Beautiful Ride" to the right of the swirl. Emboss the double outline from Jayne's large alphabet plate to frame the piece.

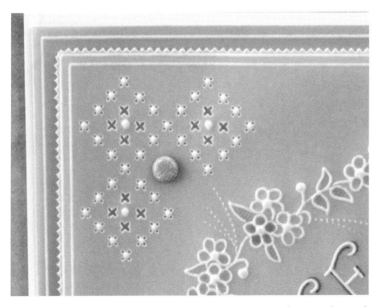

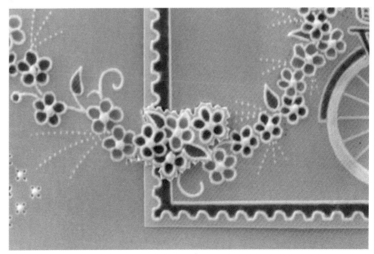

4 Using the 4-needle patterns, position underneath each corner and perforate shallow using the 4-needle tool (as coloured example). Emboss, re-perforate and cut out, following the embossing and cutting pattern.

5 On the back, shadow write behind the script using felt tip pen. Perforate with a 2-needle tool and cut around some of the flowers at the beginning of the swirl, in order to slot in the edge of the rectangle. Perforate with a 2-needle tool around the outer border and cut out. Make a larger square from the coloured parchment paper. Layer with white card and Sweet Dreams designer paper. Attach with brads.

Perforating Tools Used

2 Needle
PER-TO-70037-XX
(10261)

Pattern Map

2-needle and 3-needle perforating tools
Star tools 2mm, wheel

Christmas In Blue

Project Difficulty 1 - Easiest

Ingredients

Woven Wreath plate
Hearty Wreath plate
Nested Squares Extension and Small Alphabet Frame plate
Blendable pencils
Dorso oil or other blending solution
2-needle perforating tool
Embossing tools
Pergamano Brads x 4
Shades of blue Groovi parchment
Sticky ink
Pergamano mapping pen
Pergamano Glitters

To Make

1 Emboss the square frame using the nested squares extension. Emboss the Christmas spray from the Woven Wreath plate and the decorative swirls from the Hearty Wreath plate. Emboss a sentiment of your choice.

2 Using your embossing tools, emboss the flowers, berries and rose hips.

3 On the back of the parchment, colour the bow, leaves, pine cones and flowers with the colour of your choice.

4 Using the mapping pen, add the sticky ink to some well-chosen areas. Leave to dry and then add the glitter.

5 Perforate around the areas within the scroll work and around the outer border using the 2-needle tool. Cut out around these perforations.

6 Mat and layer using two shades of blue parchment and white card. On the second layer, add more sticky ink and glitter through the apertures.

Perforating Tools Used

2 Needle
PER-TO-70037-XX
(10261)

5 in a Circle
PER-TO-70025-XX
(10223)

Pattern Map

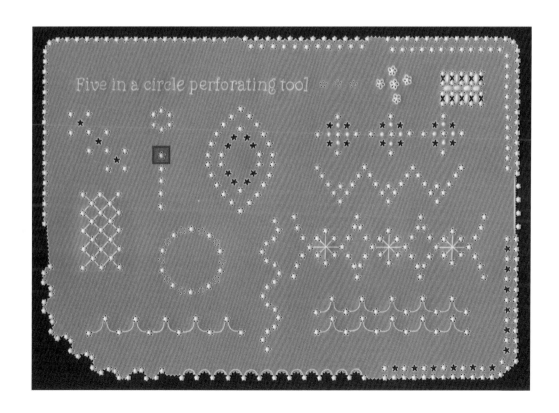

Project Difficulty 1 - Easiest

Ingredients

Nested Scallops Rectangles Groovi plate
Ribbons & Bows A5 Square Groovi plate
Twiggy Wreath A4 Square Groovi plate
Just to Say Line Sentiments Groovi border plate
2-needle perforating tool
Five in a circle perforating tool
Embossing tools
Gold Pergamano brads x 4
Ivory, Light ivory and ordinary Groovi parchment
Gold Mica paste
Pergamano mapping pen
Perga liners

To Make

1   Using plain parchment paper to make the top layer, emboss the third largest rectangle scallop frame from the Groovi plate.

On Ivory parchment, emboss the second rectangle scallop frame from the outside edge to make the middle layer. Also emboss the dots around the edge of these scallops.

2   On the top layer, emboss the Happy Christmas Sentiment and a bow of your choice. Add a line in the gaps to divide the space into two. On the lower half, emboss some flowers and swirls. In each scallop, perforate shallow with the five in a circle tool.

3   In a small pot, dilute a small amount of the Mica Gold with an equal amount of water. Using the mapping pen, trace a shadow on the Happy Christmas and the adjoining line, scrolls and flowers. Also, using a ruler and the mapping pen, draw straight lines within the embossed border, but only if you are confident enough! Using neat Mica Gold and an embossing tool, add dip dots to the flower centres, scrolls and bow. Leave to dry.

4   With a light brown or peach pencil, colour the flowers and bow lightly on the back of the parchment. Blend lightly if necessary. Using your embossing tools, emboss the tiny leaves, dots and flower centres. Emboss a dot in the centre of each five in a circle perforation. Perforate deep with the five in a circle tool, or alternatively use a 1-needle tool. Perforate around the top layer using the 2-needle tool. Cut out around these perforations.

5   Cut out around the middle layer using a guillotine or a ruler and a craft knife. Mat and layer these pieces with Light Ivory parchment and white and gold card stock. Hold in place with Pergamano brads.

Perforating Tools Used

2 Needle
PER-TO-70037-XX
(10261)

Semi-Circle Mini
PER-TO-70034-XX
(10237)

Moon
PER-TO-70031-XX
(10232)

Pattern Map

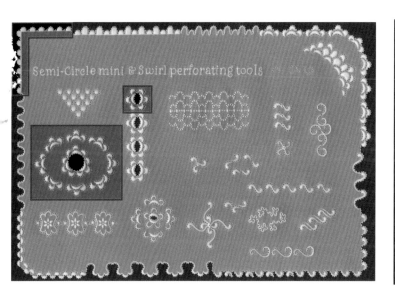

Wedding Day Wishes

Project Difficulty 3 - Advanced

To Make

1   Top Layer - On plain parchment, emboss the second heart from the outside edge. Emboss some flowers, buds and leaves, leaving a space in one corner. Middle Layer - On baby pink parchment, emboss the sixth and seventh square in from the outside edge. Emboss random words of your choice on the parts that will not be covered by the heart. Tag – On a spare piece of ordinary parchment, emboss the fourth heart from the centre. On this emboss the initials of the happy couple.

Ingredients

Jayne's Roses A5 Square Groovi Plate
Nested Squares Extension & Alphabet Frame A4 Square Groovi Plate
Nested Hearts A5 Square Groovi Plate
Wedding Dangles A5 Groovi Plate
2-needle perforating tool
Semi-circle mini perforating tool
Moon or 1-needle perforating tool
Embossing tools
White Pergamano brads x 3
Baby Pink and ordinary Groovi parchment
Perga liners

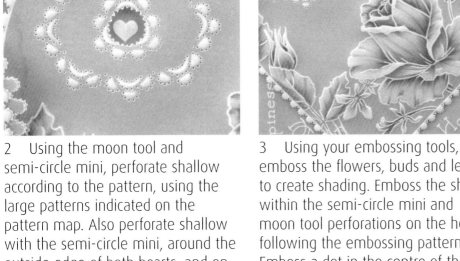

2   Using the moon tool and semi-circle mini, perforate shallow according to the pattern, using the large patterns indicated on the pattern map. Also perforate shallow with the semi-circle mini, around the outside edge of both hearts, and on each outer corner of the square (11 repeats).

3   Using your embossing tools, emboss the flowers, buds and leaves to create shading. Emboss the shapes within the semi-circle mini and moon tool perforations on the hearts, following the embossing pattern. Emboss a dot in the centre of the semi-circle mini perforations around the square.

4   With pink and green pencils, colour the flowers, leaves and buds on the back of the parchment. Then add some colour on the front for added depth, taking care not to colour over the white embossed lines.

5   Re-perforate everything with the semi-circle mini and moon tools, or use a 1-needle tool. Using the 2-needle tool, perforate along the straight lines between the semi-circle mini corners of the square. Cut out around all outer perforations, also within the centre of the lacework pattern.

6   Place the top heart layer on the middle layer, and with a white pencil mark the position of the cut out within the lacework. Emboss a tiny heart here using the Wedding Dangle plate.

7   To complete the tag, place the small heart on a scrap of Baby Pink parchment. Using the semi-circle mini, perforate around, staggering the perforations. Cut out this larger heart. Layer the two pieces and hold in place with a Pergamano brad. Finally, mat and layer your card.

Perforating Tools Used

2 Needle
PER-TO-70037-XX
(10261)

3 Needle
PER-TO-70038-XX
(10281)

4-Needle
PER-TO-70036-XX
(10251)

Flower
PER-TO-70018-XX
(10211)

Swirl
PER-TO-70032-XX
(10235)

Pattern Map

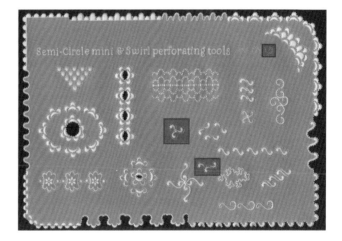

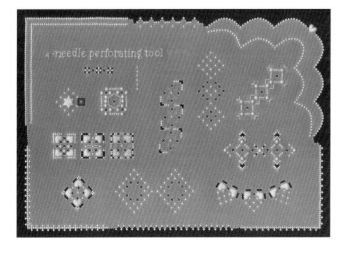

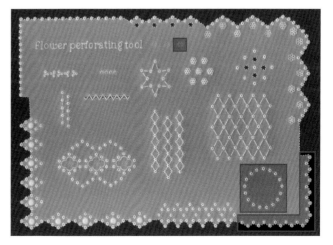

Project Difficulty 3 - Advanced

Ingredients

Nested Circles & Frilly Frames plate
Oooh-La-La Bra plate
Funky Henna Groovi border Plate
Tina's Henna Corners 2 plate
Beauty & Hope Word Chains border plate
Blendable pencils
Dorso oil or other blending solution
2-needle perforating tool
3-needle perforating tool
4-needle perforating tool
Flower perforating tool
Swirl perforating tool
Wheel embossing tool
Star 2mm embossing tool
Various ball embossing tools
Pergamano Brads x 3
Perga colours exclusive
Clarity 'Brighton Rock' designer paper

To Make

1 Emboss the fourth circle from the middle of the Nested Circles and Frilly Frame plate. Remove from plate. Roughly mark the middle of the circle with a dot, using a white pencil and a ruler.

2   Using the Oooh-La-La Bra plate, emboss a wavy line from the center dot to the edge of the circle. Turn the plate around to emboss the other half of the wavy line. This gives a nice smooth curve as shown in the picture. Alternatively, you can use a white pencil to trace the curve from the pattern on page 103. Then emboss this curve and rub out the pencil line.

3   Add a circle in each section to give a Yin & Yang effect. Using the various Henna plates, fill in one section of the circle only, avoiding the small circle.

4   Using felt tip pens, colour the Henna elements on the back of the parchment. Dorso the other half of the circle.

5   Using the multi needle tools listed and the patterns of your choice, perforate shallow within the design. With the 2-needle tool, perforate around the outside edge of the large circle.

6   Emboss using the Wheel and Star 2mm. With the appropriate embossing tools, emboss within the needle tool perforations. Re-perforate and then cut out around the outer 2-needle perforations.

7   To make the square parchment layer, use ordinary parchment paper. Take a copy of the flower tool border pattern, secure the parchment on top and perforate shallow with the flower tool. Emboss and then perforate deep.

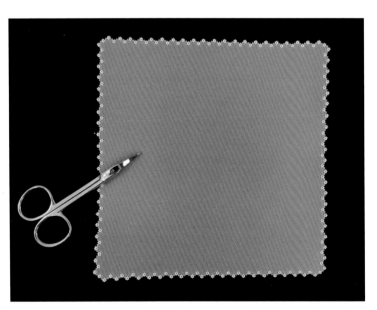

8   Cut out around the outer perforations.

9   Using the Word Chains, emboss words of your choice on the circle and the square. Mat and layer onto Brighton Rock designer paper and white card.

Photocopy this pattern to
try the card for yourself.

Yin & Yang Pattern

TOP TIPS!

1. Rub over the tumble dryer sheet on the back of your work before perforating.

2. Always perforate shallow to begin with (on a shallow perforating mat) if you are planning to add embossing in the design. Then re-perforate (on the thicker perforating mat), putting the needles into the parchment deeper this time.

3. When you are perforating, if your needle tools appear to be dragging or catching on the paper, place a tumble dryer sheet underneath your work between the pattern and the perforating mat. This will help to lubricate the needles. Alternatively, you can dip your needles into Pergasoft.

4. Keep your needle tools upright when perforating, otherwise the holes will be uneven and make cutting more difficult.

5. Make sure you can see what you are doing, using a good pair of glasses and a magnifier if necessary.

6. Make sure that your line of sight is correct so that you can see exactly what you are perforating and where. You may have to turn your paper several times when going around corners or when doing complicated patterns. Don't guess, make sure you can see!

7. Always do a test perforation on a waste piece of parchment to ensure that the needle tool is correctly aligned before you perforate your actual piece of work. Then maintain the position of the tool in your hand as you move over to your piece of work.

8. For a nice round dot, work gently from side to side, then up and down, until you feel the paper beginning to give. Now go round and round. This avoids a black dot in the middle.

9. If you trace a shape for embossing within lacework, rub the pencil out gently after the first emboss. If you leave it until later you will flatten all your work.

10. Remember you can emboss dots, shapes and also lines and curves to join up the patterns.

11. You can fit a dot in the smallest of places, even between the perforations of two needles, using the 1mm ball tool very carefully.

12. You can cut within your needle perforations, or around the outside, or both.

13. Nice lacework doesn't always have to have cutting within. If you are not confident, just perforate and emboss.

14. Don't limit yourself to a particular needle tool, combine them to make amazing patterns.

Questions & Answers

Q Do I have to cut with a twist?
A   No. Some people can get a nice picot point without twisting the scissors, whereas others get a neater result if they do.

Q My cut edge doesn't look neat, it looks really tatty! Why?
A   Check that your scissors are positioned over the waste parchment when you cut. This way the picots will be left on your work and the tatty edge will be on the waste parchment. Check your waste piece; if it has fairly neat points on it, your scissors are in the wrong position!

Q Why do some of my picot points look untidy?
A   The fact that you have some tidy points is encouraging. You must be doing something right! Try cutting a little slower, until you have perfected the technique, and then speed up as you get the hang of it. Also, make sure you have a good view of every cut, and always turn your parchment and not your scissors.

Q Cutting mat or no cutting mat?
A   It's entirely up to you. Some people like to snip with the parchment held in their hand whilst others like to snip with the parchment flat on a cutting mat.

Q   Is there a right side and a wrong side on the parchment paper?
A   No there isn't. But once you have started working on your parchment paper, embossing etc, then there will be. The general rule is that we emboss on the back and perforate from the front. If you are having trouble and get confused, then before you start, write "RIGHT" on a corner of the parchment that will not affect your design. If you can read what you have written, you will know it is the right side up.

Q My parchment sometimes rips when I am cutting it! Why is this?
A   Make sure that when you insert the points of your scissors into the perforated holes, you are not pushing them in too far. Only the very tip of the point should be used.

Q How do I get a neat embossed shape using the Star 2mm embossing tool?
A   When using this tool, it is best to place your parchment right side down, onto a hard piece of cardboard. Locate the tool in an upright position, and then pressing firmly, swivel the tool on its axis, so that each little point around the edge of the tool makes a sharp imprint on the parchment. Swivel around the tool just once, otherwise you may end up with a blurred imprint. Practise with different pressures to see which gives you the best effect.

Q How do I use the wheel embossing tool?
A   Like the Star tool, the wheel is best used on a piece of hard cardboard. This tool creates a fine broken line. Use it much like you would a pastry cutter. Place your parchment face down on the piece of cardboard and then using a little pressure roll the wheel over your parchment in the area you wish to decorate.

Notes